Let Them Eat Chaos

KATE TEMPEST was born in London in 1985. Her work includes the plays *Wasted, Glasshouse* and *Hopelessly Devoted*; the poetry collections *Everything Speaks in its Own Way* and *Hold Your Own*; the albums *Balance, Everybody Down* and *Let Them Eat Chaos*; the long poem *Brand New Ancients*; and the novel *The Bricks that Built the Houses*. She was nominated for the Mercury Music Prize for *Everybody Down*, and received the Ted Hughes Award and a Herald Angel award for *Brand New Ancients*.

D1102590

Kate Tempest

Let Them Eat Chaos

PICADOR

The musical publishing rights to the album *Let Them Eat Chaos* are owned by Domino Publishing Company Limited

First published 2016 by Picador
an imprint of Pan Macmillan
20 New Wharf Road, London N1 9RR
Associated companies throughout the world
www.panmacmillan.com

ISBN 978-1-5098-3000-8

3 5 7 9 8 6 4 2

A CIP catalogue record for this book is available from the British Library.

Printed and bound by CPI Group (UK) Ltd, Croydon, CR0 4YY

Visit **www.picador.com** to read more about all our books
and to buy them. You will also find features, author interviews and
news of any author events, and you can sign up for e-newsletters
so that you're always first to hear about our new releases.

Let Them Eat Chaos

This poem was written to be read aloud

Without contraries is no progression.

– William Blake, *The Marriage of Heaven and Hell*

There is no fear in love; but perfect love casteth out fear:
because fear hath torment. He that feareth
is not made perfect in love.

– John 4:18 (KJV)

Picture a vacuum

An endless and unmoving blackness

Peace

Or the absence, at least
of terror

Now,
in amongst all this space,
see that speck of light in the furthest corner,
gold as a pharaoh's deathbox

Follow that light with your tired eyes.
It's been a long day, I know, but look –

watch as it flickers
then roars into fullness

Fills the whole frame.
Blazing a fire you can't bear the majesty of

Here is our Sun!
And look – see how the planets are dangled around it
and held in their intricate dance?
There is our Earth.

Our
Earth.

Its blueness soothes the sharp burn in your eyes,
its contours remind you of

love.

That soft roundness.
　　　　The comfort of ocean and landmass.

Picture the world.

Older than she ever thought that she'd get.
　　　　She looks at herself as she spins.
　　　　Arms loaded with the trophies
　　　　　　　　of her most successful child.

The pylons and mines,

the power-plants shimmer in her still, cool breath.

Is that a smile
playing across her lips?

Or is it a tremor of dread?

The sadness of mothers
as they watch the fate of their children

unfold.

In now.

In

fast.

Visions.

The colours like drugs in your belly,

churning.

Your skin pulled loose as a pup's,
shaken
then tightened.
Now everything's flashing.

The waves are magnified as they roll up

towards you

And you're tiny as sand,
just a speck.

[3]

As you approach the surface
all of that

peace

that you felt is replaced with this
furious
neverknown
passion.

You're *feeling*.

The people. The life.
Their faces are bright in your body.
You're *feeling*.
You want to be close to them.
Closer.

These are your species,
your kindred.

Where have you landed?

Uncurl yourself.

Stand up and look at your limbs.

All intact.
Clothed in the fashion of the hour.

This is a city.
Let's call her

London.

And these
are the only
times

you have known.

Is this what it's come to?
You think

*What am I to make
of all this?*

At any given moment in the middle of a city
there's a million epiphanies occurring,
in the blurring of the world beyond the curtain

and the world within the person
There's a quivering.
The litter in the alleyway is singing.

People meet by chance, fall in love, drift apart again.
Underage drinkers walk the park and watch the dark descend.
The workers watch the clocks, fiddle with their Parker pens
while the grandmothers haggle with the market men.

Here, where the kids play and laugh until they fall apart,
it's kiss-chase and dancing
till it's mistakes and darkened rooms.
Too fast too soon
too slow too long
We move around all day
but can't
move
on

Is anybody else awake?
Will it ever be day again?

Overflowing plant pots.
Fence-posts.
Decorated door numbers.

Motorbike beneath a tarp.
Beaten-up Punto.

Goalposts painted on that green garage door.

There's a rainbow on that wheelie bin.
There's stickers in that window.

Smart flats. Rough flats.
Can't-get-enough-cat flats,
you know, seventeen cat-flaps.
Rich flats, broke flats.
New flats.
Old flats.
Luxury bespoke flats.
And this-has-got-to-be-a-joke flats.

Pensioners, toddlers.
Immigrants and Englishmen.
Family with six kids.
Single businesswoman.

Everybody's here trying to make or scrape a living.
The fox freezes on the alley wall and stands still, sniffing.

Bare branches sway in the front garden.
The lionmouth door knocker flaps in the breeze.
Streetlights glint on the *Beware of the Dog* sign.
The beer cans and crisp packets dance with the dead leaves.
It's 4:18 a.m.
At this very moment, on this very street,
seven different people in seven different flats
are wide awake.

Can't sleep.

Of all these people in all these houses,
only these seven are awake.

They shiver in the middle of the night
counting their sheepish mistakes.

Is anybody else awake?
Will it ever be day again?

Is anybody else
awake?

Will it ever be day
again?

We start on the corner,
with our backs against the wall
next to the old phone box
where the tramp leaves his bedding.

The road runs ahead of you
Houses and flats either side.
Walk down it;
go past the yard with the caravans,
there behind the hedges.

In the house opposite:
black gate-post
with the concrete frog squatting on top of it.

Through the hallway,
ancient wallpaper,
nicotine gold.

Up the stairs, rickety,
loaded with history.
Here in the top flat – flowers on the windowsill,
little breeze
fluttering the petals
as they stare out at the city streets.

Jemma is awake.
What woke her?
Open eyes.
Streetlights float slowly through broken blinds.

She watches as the light plays across the tattered carpet,
and she holds herself tight in the room's half-darkness.
It's cold.
She wedges her hands underneath her armpits,

It's 4:18.

And Jemma's thinking

Before I was an adult, I was a
little wreck,
peddling whatever I could get
my grubby mitts on.

Ketamine for breakfast,
bad girls for drinking with.
I gave them puppy-dog eyes
for the acid on their fingertips.

Heads in the bass bin.
Lips without faces,
getting feisty,
halfbaked in the bakery
eating pastries.

Desperate for a body
who could save me.
But I never really wanted
what they gave me.

Boiling in the chill of the dawn.
Sweating in the dole queue.
Spitting like a villain in a pantomime,
old shoes,
bad teeth.

Drinking in the rain
with my ghosts,
sitting in the back of the class,
comatose.

Villains on my back in the dark
hold me close,
but you never held.
I did some things I swore I'd never tell.
That night you tried to kill me,
run me down with your car in the snow.
I didn't realize
how far you would go.

Every day I've lived
lives in the day
I wake up in.

My dreams are all screaming and fucked
but I'm fine now.

Happiness reigns
it's carts pulling me.
Yeah, my future is bright
but my past's trying to ruin me.

> *Tried to change it*
> *but I know,*
> *if you're good to me,*
> *I will let you go.*

Tried to fight it
but I'm sure
if you're bad to me
I will like you more.

I saw some things
when I was young
that made me
who I would become

I feel them with me
every day
coz if you try
and run away

They run beside you
pace for pace
trip you up
and drag your face

Through the mud
of every wasted chance
and every
bitter taste.

My heart is sprayed up
with the names
of all my friends
who lost their way

It doesn't change,
it all remains,
it eats your strength
and feeds your shame

All I want
is someone great,
to make me
everything I ain't

But the only
ones for me
are the ones
that shouldn't be.

Even though
I'm doing good,
I'm working hard,
the work is strong

It might be fun,
just for a while,
to go back where
my hurt is from

And rinse myself
to emptiness
and push
my body close

To anybody
that can recognize
the presence
of my ghosts.

Tried to change it but I know
if you're good to me I will let you go.

Tried to fight it but I'm sure
if you're bad to me I will like you more.

In the basement flat by the garages
where the people dump their mattresses
Esther's in her kitchen, making sandwiches

The slats on her blinds are all wonky and skewed
You can see her from the street
before she moves out of view
to kick her boots off tired feet

She wipes her forehead with her wrist
She's just back from a double shift
Esther's a carer
doing nights

Behind her
on the kitchen wall
is a black and white picture
of swallows in flight

Her eyes are sore
her muscles ache
She cracks a beer
and swigs it

she holds it
to her thirsty lips
and necks it
till it's finished.

It's 4:18 a.m. again.
Her brain is full
from all she's done that day
She knows
that she won't sleep a wink
before the sun
is on its way.

She's worried 'bout the world tonight.

She's worried all the time.
She don't know how
she's supposed
to put it

       from her mind . . .

Europe is lost
America lost
London is lost
And still we are clamouring victory.

All that is meaningless rules
And we have learned nothing from history.

People are dead in their lifetimes
Dazed in the shine of the streets.
But look how the traffic's still moving.

The system's too slick to stop working.
Business is good.
And there's bands every night in the pubs,
And there's two-for-one drinks in the clubs.

We scrubbed up well
We washed off the work and the stress
now all we want's some excess.
Better yet: a night to remember
that we'll soon forget.

All of the blood that was shed for these cities to grow,
all of the bodies that fell
The roots that were dug from the earth
so these games could be played –
I see it tonight
in the stains
on my
hands.

The buildings are screaming
I can't ask for help –
        nobody knows me.
Hostile. Worried. Lonely.
We move in our packs
        and these are rites we were born to
Working and working
so we can be all that we want,
then dancing the drudgery off
But even the drugs have got boring.
Well,
sex is still good
        when you get it.

        To sleep, to dream, to keep the dream in reach.
        To each a dream.
        Don't weep, don't scream.

        Just keep it in,
        keep sleeping in.
        What am I gonna do to wake up?

I feel the cost of it pushing my body
like I push my hands into pockets,
and softly I walk and I see it:
        this is all we deserve.
The wrongs of our past have resurfaced
despite all we did to
        vanquish the traces

my very language is tainted
with all that we stole to control and erase and replace
in a country still rich with the profits of slavery.
As yet, there's been no reparations.

We clothe the corpse of our culture
parade it as *Great Britain*,
hark back to dead times and dead thinking
Call on the pillars of dead men
stifled and unloving.
No isle is an island
unsure and divided
just one little clod off the mainland, sinking.

     I am quiet

Feeling the onset of riot.

But riots are tiny
     though systems are huge
Traffic keeps moving,
     proving
     there's nothing to do.

Coz it's big business, baby,
and its smile is hideous.
Top-down violence.
Structural viciousness.

Your kids are dosed up
on prescriptions and sedatives.

But don't worry 'bout that, man.
Worry 'bout

                terrorists.

The water level's rising!

The water level's rising!

The animals –
        the polar bears
                the elephants are dying.
STOP CRYING START BUYING!!

        But what about the oil spill?

        Shh.
        No one likes a party-pooping spoilsport.

Massacres massacres massacres/new shoes
ghettoized children murdered in daylight
by those employed to protect them.
Porn live-streamed to your pre-teen's bedrooms.
Glass ceiling. No headroom.
Half a generation live beneath the breadline –
oh but it's Happy Hour on
the high street!
        Friday night at last, lads,
my treat!
        All went fine till that kid got glassed in the last bar, place went

nuts – you can ask our Lou – it was madness, road ran red, pure claret. And about these immigrants? I can't stand them. Now, mostly, I mind my own business. But they're only coming over for the benefits.

England!

England!

The blood of my kinsmen.

And you wonder why kids want to die for religion?

It goes:

Work all your life for a pittance,
maybe you'll make it to manager
pray for a raise
cross the beige days
off on your beach-babe calendar.

The Anarchists are desperate for something to smash
Scandalous pictures of glamorous rappers in fashionable magazines
– who's dating who?
politico cash in an envelope
caught sniffing lines
off a prostitute's prosthetic tits,
and it's back to the House of Lords
with slapped wrists.
They abduct kids
and fuck the heads of dead pigs,
but him in the hoodie with a couple of spliffs –

jail him
or deport him.
      It's the
            Boredofitall Generation
      the product of product placement
      and manipulation,
      shoot 'em up, brutal
      duty of care,
      come on! new shoes!
      beautiful hair.

                    bullshit

            saccharine

        ballads

      and selfies

      and selfies

      and selfies

here's me outside the palace of ME!

construct a self and psychosis
meanwhile the people are dead in their droves
but nobody noticed

well actually

some of them noticed.
You could tell by the emoji they posted.

Sleep like a gloved hand covers our eyes
The lights are so nice and bright

and let's dream

But some of us are stuck

like stones
in a
slow stream

What am I gonna do to wake up?

We are lost we are lost we are lost we are lost we are lost we are lost
we are lost we are lost we are lost
wearelostwearelostwearelost

We
Are

Lost

we are lost

we are lost
And still nothing
will stop
Nothing pauses

We have ambitions
and friendships
and our courtships
to think of
divorces to drink off
the thought of

The Money
      The Money
            The Oil.

The planet is shaking and spoiled.
Your life is a plaything. A garment to soil.

    The Toil

      The Toil.

I can't see an ending at all.

      Only

    The End.

How is this something to cherish?
When the tribesmen are dead in their deserts
to make room for alien structures?

Develop

Develop

Kill What You Find if it Threatens You.

No trace of love
in the hunt
for the
bigger buck.

Here
in the land
where nobody
gives a fuck.

What am I gonna do
to wake up?

Across the street, above the green
in the flat with the colourful curtains
Alicia's wrapped in her blankets
Head leant back on the wall

She's gripping her knees.
Looking for purpose.
Shaking and nervous.

She keeps a brave face on all day long
but now the brave face is gone.

Something in the changing seasons
prickled in her skin all day
Sucked her back through time
and left her feeling far away.

He was in her dream.

She hasn't dreamed of him for months.
She's so tired when she sleeps,
she doesn't really dream at all.

But there he was:

holding his belly,
blood on his shirt.

She heard him scream her name.
And then she saw him fall.

Alicia wipes her face
and whispers to herself
was just a dream

She sniffs and nods and dries her eyes.
She checks the time.

It's 4:18.

It's a strange thing.
Your face seems to fade with the changing seasons.
Then, for some reason
it comes back
more present than ever.

Well not your face, really.
More a sense of you.
Even though I know it's happened
it's no more comprehensible

than if it was an abstract thing.
Someone else's friend.

Are you asking me for something?
Is there something I should do?

It's hard on your mother.
She lost your little brother too.
But your sister's doing good.
She's smart.
Smart like you.

She'll finish her degree next year.
Try and find a job I s'pose.
She's got her head screwed on right.
You don't have to worry.

But is there something else?
I mean, if there is, I'm sorry.

I can't really think
what you might want from me.

I heard your voice so loud it woke me up.

I don't believe in ghosts.

Work's fine. Life's good.
Ty's nearly four now.
Smart enough to walk round
and hear what I don't say.

The night it happened
is vivid in my brain.

It won't fade.

Life is long, still.
Some things don't change.

Be nice to fall in love again.
But that ain't gonna happen soon.
Trying to get some money saved,
fix up the living room.

I nearly got in trouble
I got angry with my manager.
There's this young girl who works with us.
He tried to put his hands on her.

It's such a waste.
So many idiots alive and kicking.
Why'd it have to be the only sane man in town?
I'm probably only saying that
coz you're not around.

I'm keeping my chin up.
I don't let it get me down.

I heard your voice so loud it woke me up.

I don't believe in ghosts.

You're with me all the time.

I think I know you better
than I did when we were hanging out together.

What's it like where you've gone?
Well I can feel it, it's ok.
I know you can't say.

But you've been with me all day.

I have to tell you

When it happened, I couldn't cry for ages.
But when it hit me
I fucking screamed like a lion in a cage.
And look, I fasted.
I didn't eat a thing for like a week –
I just walked across the heath in the rain
Spitting bars to the grass
Listening to the cars
skidding past.

I thought life would get more real or something.
More fast.

But it didn't.

When I look at your son, though, life's hidden
meanings come to the front of my vision.

And it's weird.
The way I see it right now, it's so strong.
      I'd never be the person I've become if you had never gone.

      Everything's connected. Right?
        Everything's connected.

And even if I can't read it right, everything's a message.

We die.
So others can be born.

We age
so others can be young.

The point of life is live.
Love if you can. Then pass it on.

We die so others can be born
      We age so others can be young
         The point of life is live,
           Love if you can
             Then pass it on.

Now, who's this staggering home?
Jabbering,
looking like some streetsmart arrogant gnome?
Feet sticking to the kerb like javelins thrown,
gesturing wildly,

having full blown
conversations with himself,
saying, *haven't you grown?* to his face in the windows,
grimacing
        grappling with half a cigarette
                not managing.

This is Pete.
Pete grew up on this street.
He moved away
but he's back living at his Dad's so he can save.

He rigs stages at live events
But every time he gets paid
        he gets wasted
and wakes up with less than he made
        and he hates it
But that's life, right?
        Fast-paced, shit-faced, low-maintenance.

And all of his mates
are kind of on the same page
        it's basic wages,
takes ages
to get through the month
        then payday comes
and it's drinks all round.
        Outrageous behaviour,
living right now
and no sense of later.

Pills by the pocketful.
      Nights last days.
          And even if he never splashed out
he still couldn't make the rent on his own place.

      Face it.

It's 4:18
      Pete's fourteen doors from home.
          His thoughts are like a pack of starving dogs,
Fighting
      over
          the
             last
                bone.

      No no no no no no no. Yeah, so anyway,
what was I saying?
      Fuck it mate. Hold on. I'm coming up,

wait
      Good night,
          weren't it?
                Must have been

      Burnt too
          much on the
      good stuff,
          lucky me.

I looked up,
saw my future
        unravel in the lights,
funny innit?

I'll have that sinking feeling any minute.
            But you can't win a race
        less you're running in it,
    right?

        Can't get a taste 'less you've taken a bite.

    Man
    I'm
    climbing
    the
    walls,

    things are getting difficult

    it's all

    take take take

            I start early,
        work late.

    Putting in the hours
        for these drugs tokens.

Love's a joke
        till your blood's pulsing

Love is real
        when you start choking

I'm double dropping
        in the vast ocean

State of me, mate.
Blatantly the way I was made.

Man, I been getting on it
        since back in the day.

Good place for a bad time
if you ask me.
Trust me
Nothing gets past me.
Bad place for a good time,
know what I mean?
I never met no one like you,

it feels like a dream.

Woops.
Back here again.
How many times have I sworn it's the end?

Woops.
I know *this* feeling.
Shovelling the rubbish till I'm staring at the ceiling.

Woops.
Dancing to a shit tune.
Hands in the air when it hits you.

Woops.
I'm lying in my bed
and my brain is eating my head.

I got these demons that I can't shake
My past is a vast place.
Can't get away.
Life got grim back then,
like it does.
You know how it feels
to lose people you love?

I like talking to you like this!
You wanna come back?
Couple drinks,
something like that?

I got a gram on my nightstand,
I got an eighth of squidgy black.
I got this feeling that we're gonna be
friends.

I got this song
                I wanna play it to you.
I got this dream
                I'm gonna make it happen.
I got this thing,
                I wanna say it to you.

I been writing poems,
                it's a thing that I do,
would you mind if I
shared one with
                you?

No. Course not.

Right.

Sorry.

This time of night,
I always end up spouting
the same old shite.

Reminds me of this time I was trying to find my mind in the
back of this rave. This kid was spilling blood all over the place. And I was
looking out for someone to save or be saved by, and I found this paper
plate. I started writing,
                man, it felt fucking great.

I knew then
                me and the pen
                                we were one and the same.

But I can't take the strain of the days
I'm pretty sure I'm halfway
to insane

You've got such a nice face
And your eyes are like
rain
I'd try and kiss you
if I could just remember your

                    name

        Woops.
        Back here then s'pose.
        Don't watch the state of my nose.

        Woops.
        My jaw's gone west.
        I've started getting pains in my chest
            Is that normal?

        Woops.
        There goes my promise.
        All it took was two drinks
            till I got on it.

        Woops.
        I swear this person isn't me.
        We did have fun though,
            didn't we?

        Didn't we?

Above Pete's head
        as he fumbles with his key
The clouds get dark,
        start brawling.
        Wargames
        ancient faces,
pushing each other around.
                The sky's changing.

A roaring storm is coming.
        A howling mist,
        a growling downpour.

But Pete don't see it.
        Pete's too busy
        trying to make
        his key fit.

                Can't.
                Quite.
                Get.
                It.

                        Right.

In their rooms, Alicia,

                and Esther

                and Jemma

are too concerned with their own thoughts
                              to think about the weather.

But we see —
              the clouds like furious ink
              thick liquid sinks and
              whips the wind
              pitch-shifted
              rumble, screams from a swollen grin —

there's a big storm rolling in.

              We came from the four corners
              We are the raw waters that course
              The four horsemen will drink
              from the water that pours

              We carry the river,
                      the reservoir
                          the residue
                              the rising waves,
                      the sea spray,
                              the inevitable churn and crush

              Many voices in our vapours,
                              we surge and gush —
                          we were steam
                      in a distant heat

[39]

We moved rapid over landscapes,
                gathering speed
                        Desertland. City. Forest and beach.

Heading for the people asleep.

                        Ready to bleed
                        Unleash the torrents.
                                Come clean.

        Made of many lessons.
        Pouring down.
        But you better learn to swim
        before you drown.

Hard rain falling,
on all the half-hearted
half-formed
fast walking
Half-fury, half-boredom.
Hard talking.
Half-dead from exhaustion.
Hard pushed,
but the puddles keep forming.
                        Don't fall in.

                Some saw us in their tea-leaves
                Some felt us in their knees
                Most left it to the weathermen
                to tell them there was nothing to see.

You can play dumb and ignore for so long
But we've been in the mountains getting strong
We've seen you
      filling up the sky with your fumes
Sitting in your rooms
      like you're all that ever lived
Heads down to the lives
      of the others in your towns
Running from the rains
      like you've never been kissed

Look – leave
      your possessions and funds
      tell your friends that you've gone
      to make peace with the things you've never done.
      Come dance in the deluge
      Spill like the flood.

The weather-vane swings
      things will never change sing
            All the money men who close their eyes
                and pretend
that this rumble
      must be low planes.

           So strange

Hard rain falling
on all the half-hearted, half-formed, fast walking
half-fury, half-boredom,
hard talking.

Half-dead from exhaustion,
hard pushed but the
                    puddles keep forming.
                              Don't fall in.

And they will run to the highest hill.
                    Consult the old books.
Ask the dead mystics
                    for wisdom they don't trust.
The people
          will flock to the garages,
stock-pile canisters
                    of gasoline
                    tinned fish
                    and bandages.
Count the seconds between the thunder and the lightning
Scared of every other body running round frightened.

We can't carry on like this, you will mutter
Staring with disgust
          at the people
                    weeping in the gutter.

          We made no trouble
          we played by the rules.
          I worked double shifts
          to get my kids through school.

But you were so focused
on your own little part,

you went ploughing on
blind in the dark.

                              No heart.

We are not the dread storm that will end things
We're just your playful
                gale-force friend
                        in the end times
Come to remind you
        that you're not an island
Life is much broader
        than borders
                but who can afford
                        to think over the walls of this fortress.
        Of course it's important
                to provide roof and floorboards
                        for you and yours
                and be secure in your fortunes.
        But you're more
                than the three or four
                        you'd go to war for.
        You're part of a people that need your support
        and whose world is it?
If it belongs to the corporates
        the People are left on the doorstep.
                        Door-shut.
        Nauseas.
        Tortured by all that they lost.

Hard rain falling on all the half-hearted, half-formed, fast-walking
half-fury, half-boredom, hard-talking. Half-dead from exhaustion,
hard pushed but the puddles keep forming.

Don't fall in.

On the second floor
        of the new block
                In the flat with the yellow door,
next to the boarded-up independent record store

Bradley is awake.

He's watching notches on his clock face
        Just lying there thinking.
        Limbs like fallen buildings.
Feeling like every day he's ever lived
        is out to kill him.

Bradley's got a good job; he works in PR.
He moved south a few months back.
Top-whack flat,
all mod-cons.
Wall-size windows.
Manchester boy
        done good in The Big Smoke.

Young professional, single, Tinder and flings
        Life seems simpler
                than it's ever been

he's doing well, he's

Living The Dream

And he's paying the mortgage off.
He doesn't know why
he's not sleeping at nights.

He could get up
Try and walk it off.

But he's got to get to work in a matter of hours.
Is he awake or asleep?
He can't tell,
he can't dream,
he can't feel,
he can't scream,
man,
it's 4:18

Life's just a thing that he does.

He rolls over, cold pillow, warm body,
at the end of his tether as usual,
he breathes softly,
he burrows down deep,
closes his eyes,
and he thinks, is *this* really what it means to be alive?

The days go past like pictures on a screen.
Sometimes I feel like my life
                    is someone else's dream.

Most days I'm dazed
            walking round
I'm working
            talking
            perking up.
But always feel I can't be certain
                that I've woken up
                            at all.

Is this life?
            Will this pass?

This feeling
            like I'm looking at the world
            from behind glass?

Even when I'm laughing hard
            or falling on my arse
Or half plastered
before it's even dark
Or when some hard bastard
            barges past
When I'm passing my targets at work
I can't shake the feeling
            that life hasn't started
It's worse

in the evenings at parties
I'm standing apart
My heart's hard
I can't hardly be heard,
but I'm harping on, barking out words.

Is this me?

Is this what I'm doing?

I know I exist

but I don't feel a thing

I'm eclipsed,
I'm elsewhere.

The worst part is

I don't think
that I care.

What am I gonna do to

wake up?

I know it's happening,

but who's it happening to?

Has it happened to you?

I know it's happening.

But who
    is it happening to?

Has this happened to you?

I try new things.
I shoot films on my phone.
And play them back
    when I'm alone

    – *Did* that happen?

I walk around,
    trying to understand every sound.

Trying to make my feet connect
    with every inch of ground.

The sky flattens my cap,
battens me down.
Everything in its category.

> Package and sell.
> Flattering girls,
> battle reality,
>> it's Battle Royale
> Everyone's chattering,
>> nothing is Real.

Collect my salary.

> Cooking a meal,
>> rice and vegetables.

I exercise regularly.
> How do I feel?

Whistle a melody.

> Is this

> all

> that's ahead of me?

I always thought
> that life
>> would mean more to me

eventually.

I hate to think I'll make it to seventy,
potentially
seventy-five,
And realize I've never been alive,
and spend the rest of my days
regretting,
wishing I could be
forgetting.

I know it's happening

But who's it happening to?

Has this happened to you?

I know it's happening

But who's it happening to?

Has *this* happened to *you*?

Just two doors down
in the first-floor flat
in the old ramshackle house
with the novelty doorbell,

the lights are still on.

Zoe plays her music low.
She's got a bottle on the go,
    everything's in boxes

It's been a
        long
        night
        packing.

Clothes in black bin-bags.
Blu-Tack greases the paintwork.
    What the fuck is all this stuff?
There's the road sign stolen from Quickshag Street.
Shirts and skirts
    posters, CDs,
        comedy coasters,
    broken TV.
    Birthday card that her sister made
in the distant past
    when she turned thirteen.

Hair stuff, books,
    love letters she can't bin,
and outside the night
    and inside the last hurrah.

    Limited edition Air Max One Tens
      Che Guevara Bust
complete with his ornamental glass cigar.

For years
    the landlord never fixed the shower
The mould kept growing up the kitchen walls.
    He'll do it up nice now
    sure
    repaint it.
He's tripled the rent.
    He's gonna get it and all.

Only got a few hours left
to get the room all packed and clean.

Zoe goes to the window
looks to the street
lights up a smoke

    it's 4:18.

    The squats we used to party in
        are flats we can't afford
    The dumps we did our dancing in
        have all been restored

    Pints are up two quid
        the staff are beautiful and bored
    You think it's coming round here?
        It's falling on its sword.

It don't feel like home no more
    I don't speak the lingo.
Since when was this a winery?
    It used to be the bingo.

I've walked these streets for all my life
    they know me like no other.
But the streets have changed.
    I no longer feel them
        shudder

           Alright alright, I get the gist.

     Whose city is this?

It doesn't want me no more.
I've had a glimpse
    into the future.
It stinks.

London's a walled fort,
it's all for the rich,
if you fall short
you fall.
You know where the door is.

    Board up the broken,

    do it up,
        sell it back

make it bespoke.

It's all out in the open.

It's fine, man,
hike the price right up
and smile with your friends
in the posh new nightclubs.

My streets have been dug up.
Re-paved.

New routes for commuters.

The landscape has changed

I'm looking for the old tags,
the graffs that once meant
safe territory

but it seems
every hieroglyph gets whitewashed
eventually.

All I see is
luxury tenements
woebegone residents
leisure-bent resin-heads
puffing on pleasure

Everyone reckoning
　　something is beckoning.
　　　　Never a minute here.

　　Only forever.

Towering towerblocks
Scaffolding rattling

The Tube is a battering ram
　　full of passengers

smashing its way into town.
　　We are scavengers
scrapping around in the sludge
　　for our sustenance

Paradise partylife.
　　Rubbing our shoulders
into the mould.
　　We do
　　what we're told.

We're Sisyphus pushing his boulder

The kids are alright.
　　But the kids'll get older.

And so I'm moving on. I've got it all to play for.
I'll be the invader
　　in some other neighbourhood.

I'll be sipping Perfect Coffee
        thinking, *this is pretty good,*

while the locals grit their teeth and hum
Another Fucking One Has Come.

Up the stairs: chip-fat grey and London green with damp
On the fifth floor, where the wind grips your jaw
and holds you in its clamp
there's a red door, bordered by mottled glass
and inside
a lighted lamp.

Pious lives here.

Pious is tired but can't sleep, she twitches. Wired.
She lies beside a sleeping body, a girl she barely knows.
She met her in the pub
and it went the way it goes.
        The girl's name is Rose,
But Pious is lovesick for her Thorn.
        She left her in the summer,
        and since then Pious can't get warm.
She's carried her, stuck in her side, since the day that she was born
She dreamed of her and knew her shape
long before she saw her form.

It's 4:18, and Pious
has been staring at the blinds for hours
She tells herself it's all her fault.
She doesn't love.
She just devours.

Can't sleep.
So much to do.

I'm trying to get closer to you
And you're
so far away.

I'm trying to get hold of what's true.

And what's true
isn't true
when it's day.

Tell me, how can I sleep?
Got so much to do.
I'm trying to get closer to you.
And you're so

far away.

All that I say and I do
are things
that you do
and you say.

How come I'm becoming the one
that I'm running from,
hunted by?
Slurring my words in the pub
Feeing nervous
and overexcited

Arms round the waist
of a girl who might make it alright
for a night.
Yeah, she tears me to pieces.

I lie beside her,
awake

while she sleeps
And I feel much closer
to you
than I felt
when you were still here.
Spill beer till you reappear.

I'm thinking of

you.

And the things
you do to me.

I'm thinking of

you.

And the things

You

do

to

me

Pain in my liver.
OK.

Shame. So much shame
can't bear my frame
Can't bear your name.
OK.

Can't bear this game.
Let's play.

New rules.
Old rituals.

Guilt trip.

Heartstrings snap

Want to, can't go back.

        Too Much.

                Not
                Enough.

I can't get your claws out of my guts

                I'm thinking of you. And the things you do to me.
I'm thinking of you. And the things

                You

                do

                to

                me

This is my head
GETOUTOFIT
You didn't want it.
How come you're still hanging around in it?

                This is my body LETGOOFIT
                You didn't want it.
                How come you're still fucking controlling it?

This is my night. Get lost in it.
This is my bridge. Stop crossing it.
This is my face,
stop smiling.

This is my space.
You been gone
so long

How come I still find you

hiding?

Fighting me.
I'm fighting.
The light's too sharp.
I'm frightened.
Nightmares.
Tighten
my hands
round my own throat

You're the snake charmer
and I'm the old rope.

No hope.
Just go now
please,

just leave.

You're still in the air that I breathe.

I'm stranded.
Arms outstretched for a body
        Any body
                Here's a body
                        But I wake up
                                and I can't stand 'em.

                I feel so grubby.
                        Don't want can't stop just love me
                Breath like a cigarette stubbed in the gutter
                        Come close,
                no wait –

                        don't touch me.
                Ugly.
                        Push and pull phonecall beep beep looking through
                        names for the one that feels most dangerous.

                I can't believe you're in love again.

                        I can't open my heart to anybody but

                                        strangers.

                I'm thinking of you.
                        And the things you do to me.

So: here is our moment.
Frozen.
We've seen our seven,
  unmoving
  in lonely homes.
It's been 4.18
and dawn's still
  hours off yet

My god and they are cold and listless
not quite sure that they exist
here in this moment
slow as glass
lips haunted by the ghosts of kisses.

  There is the endless saturation of the days
and here they are
  There is nothing moving
  but their breath

But watch now
  as the breaking storm outside
   animates the frozen moment.

The sky cracks into a wild-mouthed grin
and unleashes all the water that it carries
Vapour grown heavy
from every distant puddle,
  every lapping wave-tip,
   every churning river

contributing to this

    rain.

Pete on his doorstep looks up, mouth agape.
Drops his key in shock and laughs a howling ancient laugh.

The lightning charges through them
rips the sky and startles every roof into stark relief
and they see their city

    new.

Esther hears herself shout a strange bark into the silence of her kitchen.
Jemma sits bolt upright in bed wide-eyed and she stares at the rain
as it smashes itself against her window

Zoe puts her boxes down
Bradley reaches for his dressing-gown

    See it from above.

Seven doors to seven flats open at the same time
and light the raining pavement.

Seven broken hearts
Seven empty faces
heading out of doors:
Here's our seven perfect strangers.

And they see each other.

Strangely dressed, one shoe and one slipper, socks falling off, smiling,
gathering slowly, tentatively in the middle of the road.
Shielding their eyes at first
        but then
                tipping their necks back, unhunching their shoulders,
        opening their bodies up to
                        the storm
And their hair is flattened against their heads
        or puffed up madly outwards
And their hands
        slip off their chins and cheeks
        as they clutch their faces
                open-mouthed

Amazing! they shout
You seen it?! they shout

As they walk towards each other
dragging themselves like the wounded
and band close, close,
shocked and laughing,
soaked to the skin.

Joined in it, known in it
Witness to a shared thing, theirs as much as anyone's
Bones struck, ringing in chorus.

And in the morning when it's over and they start their days as usual
They will be aware of this baptism in a distant way.
It will become a thing they carry close like the photo of a dead parent
tucked always in the inside pocket
Fading like the heartbeat

Picture a vacuum

Pitch in the vacuum

Pictures and pictures and pictures

And vacuums

Indigenous apocalypse
    decimated forests.
        The winter of our discontent's
    upon us.

Desolate apostles
    slurping Strongbow at the crossroads
        We are nothing but an eating mouth
    Oesophagus colossal

Will not stop until we've beaten down
the planet into pellets
before the interstellar mission to inflict more terror.
It's killing me it's killing me
It's filling me
I'm vomiting.
it's still in me.

Everything is fine really, silly me.

Poor kids shot dead
Poor kids locked up
Poor kids saying
this is the future you left us?
Stocked up, lunchmeat
Processed punch from an unclean fat cat
Tasty tasty poison.

Carcinogenic
diabetic
asthmatic
epileptic
Post-traumatic bipolar and disaffected

Atomized

Thinking we're engaged
when we're pacified
Staring at the screen so
we don't have to see the planet die.

What we gonna do to wake up?
We sleep so deep
It don't matter how they shake us.
If we can't face it, we can't escape it

But tonight the storms come.

She's screaming, she's screaming.
The drones
turned her beautiful boy into a pile of bones
No body to bury
Nobody is home
Running from war
The boats full
The boats sinking
a mile off shore.
No beds in the hospitals
Our minds are against us

Imagine your daughter was gunned down
defenceless
on her way to school,
there'd be uproar –
but she's collateral damage.
It doesn't matter.

If our kids are fine
That's enough for us
You can't love into a vacuum.
There's got to be a limit.

Welcome to the biggest crime that's ever been committed

You think you and I are different kinds?

You're caught up in specifics.

You and I apart are easier to limit.
The illusion's so complete
it's impossible to bring it into focus.

Cinematic stock footage:
people are locusts.
Uniformed men keep unleashing explosives.

What we gonna do to
wake up?

We sleep so deep
it don't matter how they shake us.

If we can't face it
we can't escape it.
But tonight the storms come.

Tunnel vision
tunnel vision
Work drinks. Heartbreak.
Can't face the past, the past's a dark place.

Can't sleep.
Can't wake.
Sitting in our boxes

Notching up our victories
    as other people's losses.

        Another day another chance to turn your face away from pain
Let's get a takeaway
Meet me in the pub a little later
    say the same things as ever

    Life's a waiting game
When we gonna see that life is happening?

            And that every single body
        bleeding on its knees
    is an abomination?
    All things are, in their way, communicating.
We're just sparks
tiny parts
of a bigger constellation.
    Minuscule molecules
        that make up one body

            The tragedy and pain
        of a person that you've never met
                    is present in your nightmares,
        in your pull towards
                despair

The sickness of the culture
and the sickness in our hearts
is a sickness that's inflicted

by the distance
that we share.

It was our bombs that started this war.

It rages at a distance,
so we dismiss all its victims as strangers,
but they're parents and children
made dogs by the danger.
Existence is Futile so we don't engage.

It was our boats that sailed,
killed, stole and made frail
it was our boots that stamped
it was our courts that jailed
and it was our fucking banks that got bailed.

It was us who turned bleakly away,
looked back down at our nails and our wedding plans
in the face of a force 10 gale
we said *it's not up to us to make this place a better land.*

It's not up to us to make this place
a better land

Justice

Justice

Recompense

Humility

Trust is

trust is something we will never see

Till Love is unconditional

The myth of the individual

Has left us disconnected   lost
and pitiful.

I'm out in the rain
it's a cold night in London

Screaming at my loved ones
to wake up and love more.

Pleading with my loved ones to

wake up
and love more.